We acknowledge the First Nations People of this land
we now call Australia.

We acknowledge that our Sovereignty was never ceded.

We acknowledge that this land always was and always will be
the lands of the Aboriginal and Torres Strait Islander Peoples.

We acknowledge with pride the creativity, strength and
resilience of our First Nations LGBTQIA+ community and
with this publication we share an insight into our lives, our
loves, our aspirations and our world.

Sydney WorldPride provides a platform to Gather, Dream
and Amplify our voices and to celebrate together with our
Community and our Allies.

*We GATHER as a diverse yet unified mob; we DREAM and imagine
a just and fair world, and we work together to AMPLIFY (grow) our
voices and share our lived experiences as First Nations People.*

BLACKBOOKS, a division of Tranby Aboriginal Co-operative
Limited, invites you to listen deeply to the voices of our
First Nations LGBTQIA+ poets, writers and storytellers.

T0359823

**BLACK
BOOKS**

First published 2023 by
BLACKBOOKS®
a division of
Tranby Aboriginal Co-operative Limited.
Tranby.edu.au

BLACKBOOKS.online
BLACKBOOKS@tranby.edu.au

Publisher: Tony Duke

 A catalogue record for this
book is available from the
National Library of Australia

ISBN: 978-0-6454282-3-0 (pbk)

ISBN: 978-0-6454282-4-7 (epub)

ISBN: 978-0-6454282-5-4 (epdf)

Printed in Maryborough, Victoria by MacPhersons Printing Group Pty Ltd

BLACKBOOKS® is a registered trademark.

This project is supported by
Sydney WorldPride

This project is supported by the
Copyright Agency's cultural fund

 This book has been printed on paper certified by the Programme
for the Endorsement of Forest Certification (PEFC). PEFC is
committed to sustainable forest management through third party
forest certification of responsibly managed forests.

NANGAMAY
dream
MANA
gather
DJURALI
grow

**FIRST NATIONS
AUSTRALIA
LGBTQIA + POETRY**   EDITED BY
ALISON WHITTAKER & STEVEN LINDSAY ROSS

BLACK
BOOKS

CONTENTS

09   Preface

13   Foreword • Arlie Alizzi

17   Introduction • Alison Whittaker & Steven Lindsay Ross

18   #mardigrasrainbowdreaming • Jazz Money

21   Resonance • Alita Morgan

22   Awi sista! • Jacyn de Santis

23   Coming in • Sandy O'Sullivan

24   Never not thinking (about that) • Ellen van Neerven

25   Ginger • Gary Lee

25   Moon • Gary Lee

26   my grandmother's two brown hands • Bebe Backhouse

34   Love & Other Ridiculous Notions of Togetherness • Lay Maloney

37   Bubba, You're Gonna Go Home • Vika Mana

39   Gugurrgaagaa '93 Where a heart like mine belongs • Colin Kinchela

40   Easyfree • Gavin Ivey

42   Earth Mother • Samuel Barsah

43   We stand together • Ella Noah Bancroft

44   future library • Ellen O'Brien

45   Sea Glass • Neika Lehman

46   Suspended Tethering Lives • Ari Mills

48   Fat Queer Colony • Andrew Farrell

49   the humble middle ground • Dominic Guerrera

50   Éla • Gary Lee

51   Personless Love • Ari Mills

52   impossible to contain • Natalie Harkin

54   Chocolate • Steven Oliver

58   For the love of Crystal • Jacyn de Santis

60   Freedom? • John Mukky Burke

65   Everything I do I do for you • Keith Quayle

68   choreography • Bebe Backhouse

70   Dangalaba soul water • Laniyuk

72   March with Pride • Laniyuk

75   Colonial fetish – Part 1 • Latoya Aroha Rule

76   Pain • John Mukky Burke

80   How we die (for David Hardy) • Sandy O'Sullivan

82   she's gone and near • David Hardy

83   A Grass Tree by Any Other Name • Luke Patterson

84   Dream • Lay Maloney

86   My awakening eyes • Keith Quayle

88   redbellyblacksnake • Jazz Money

89   Stick together • Tyberius Larking

90   I touch the wound and it doesn't hurt
     as much as the first time • Ellen O'Brien

92   You can't pray the Gay out of me • Kirli Saunders

93   un_domesticated • Yvette Henry Holt

98   The Quiet Work • Ellen van Neerven

99   Palangalite • Steven Lindsay Ross

102 Pieman Heads • Neika Lehman

103 Fam is Blak • Latoya Aroha Rule

107 Carp • Alison Whittaker

110 Sacredness Sewn of Footprints • Elijah Manis

112 The Poets

127 Thanks

128 Notes on sources

PREFACE

NANGAMAY dream MANA gather DJURALI grow is a collection of poetry that showcases the diverse and resilient voices of our First Nations LGBTQIA+ poets, writers and storytellers from across this land we now call Australia. We acknowledge and offer special thanks to Dharug Custodian and Knowledge Holder Aunty Julie Jones for her support in sharing these Dharug words for us to use in our title.

Colonisation and Christianisation continues to impact the lives and loves of our First Nations communities and community members. Our LGBTQIA+ brothers and sisters, Mothers and Fathers, Aunties and Uncles, friends and lovers have sustained their unique identities and Cultures amidst invasion, ideas of empire, and the onslaught of western capitalist and religious beliefs and practices. For too long, we as First Nations Peoples, were told that we did not exist, we had no Culture, and that we had no connection to our ancestral lands; Country that our families and ancestors held custodial responsibilities and relationships with for millennia. In sharing this collection, we take a stand and shout outLOUD and with pride ALWAYS WAS ALWAYS WILL BE ABORIGINAL LAND.

Our hope is that our readers, both First Nations and non-Indigenous, will be enriched by this shared insight into the lives, loves, dreams, hopes, frustrations and aspirations of our First Nations LGBTQIA+ poets, writers and storytellers. In publishing this anthology, we have endeavored to maintain the authentic voice and form of each contribution. The distinctive page layouts, typography and poetic styling of each piece reflects and affirms the uniqueness and diversity of our First Nations LGBTQIA+ community.

Sydney WorldPride provides a platform to dream, gather and amplify the voices of our First Nations LGBTQIA+ community members. *NANGAMAY dream MANA gather DJURALI grow* is our contribution and offering to this international celebration of the LGBTQIA+ community.

For many years, Tranby Aboriginal Co-operative Limited (established in 1957) and BLACKBOOKS has been known as a safe and supportive place for First Nations LGBTQIA+ community members. At times it was a haven and a meeting place for many First Nations LGBTQIA+ people when they left their home communities and first ventured into Sydney seeking acceptance and understanding. In 2022 we launched the outLOUD First Nations LGBTQIA+ Story and Writing project with a series of podcasts profiling the lives and practice of First Nations LGBTQIA+ creatives from across Australia. All funds raised from the sale of this publication will go to support the ongoing work of BLACKBOOKS and the outLOUD project.

This publication is the result of many hours of work mixed with a big helping of love and respect. Our editors Alison Whittaker and Steven Lindsay Ross are to be commended for their vision and commitment that has resulted in the publication of this anthology that we now share with you and the world. Special thanks goes to Tony Duke and the BLACKBOOKS Team for their refusal to stop when things got hard and their untiring dedication to publish beautiful books – beautiful Black books.

As Australia as a nation, and we all as individuals, move along the journey of reconciliation and truth-telling with First Nations Peoples and communities, we invite you to embrace the ideas and intentions that are here so generously shared by our First Nations LGBTQIA+ poets, writers and storytellers.

In sharing this collection, we hope that you are challenged, inspired and touched by *NANGAMAY dream MANA gather DJURALI grow.*

In Unity.

Tranby Aboriginal Co-operative Limited
BLACKBOOKS
outLOUD Story and Writing Project
www.BLACKBOOKS.online/outLOUD/

FOREWORD

Situated on the brink of Sydney WorldPride on the lands of the Gadigal, Cammeraygal, Bidigal, Dharawal and Dharug, I want to take a moment to appreciate this revelatory collection of poems, *NANGAMAY dream MANA gather DJURALI grow*.

For readers unfamiliar with the history, it should be said that rather than operating from marginal spaces, the edges of the movement, First Nations people, always activist, have been at the forefront of both the celebration and resistance of Sydney's Gay and Lesbian Mardi Gras. The very first float dedicated to First Nations people led the parade in 1988. That was the year of the Australian Bicentennial, and the float acted as an opportunity to represent an historic wave of protest that has since become legendary. The First Nations float has been a staple of the proceedings of Mardi Gras – but our older generations remind us that Blak Queers have been part of the movement since long before that formal gesture in 1988.

All of this took place before I was born. Despite the pool of fearless creative Blak talent in our LGBTQIA+ communities, and the continued flourishing of and increasing presence and audience for First Nations poetic culture, LGBTQIA+, sistergirl and brotherboy poets have never before been formally anthologised in this land now called Australia. This gathering of voices is long overdue.

And it does not disappoint. The soulful hedonism, loving courage and daring radicalism of the original Sydney Mardi Gras spirit is carried out in the poetry contained in these pages. Jacyn De Santis'

Arlie Alizzi

poem 'For the love of Crystal' stands out as a definitive piece for this collection. It reads as a love letter to a Sistagal from the Tiwi Islands who might be Crystal Love, the Queen Supreme. This divine figure transitions between her responsibilities, looking after others, breaking up fights, being the big mumma. Her story refuses simple categorisation. She is a vulnerable woman, sometimes heartbroken, but also a producer of artistic alchemy. Violence hangs around her, but she is no victim; she swallows us whole.

In another poem, a small but staunch textual shrine to self-care, Ellen Van Neerven's poem 'The Quiet Work' insists against the tide of white and hetero and cis-normative Australian culture, on doing 'the quiet work / of loving myself / before it is too late'. Elsewhere, Andy Farrell promises us they will 'occupy too much space'.

There is a power and an audacity in these works. Jacyn De Santis' protagonist is a 'Big boss bitch'. In 'Everything I do I do for you' Keith Quayle writes infectiously;

I don't fear institutions
Irwin's stingray can't even fuck with me

...

I can walk barefoot on iron nails
I am immune to death
I don't need blessings because I always have good luck

It is freeing and glorious to see these expressions of unbridled sexuality, vulnerability and invincible spirit in print from First Nations poets.

The last ten years has seen an upswell in the production of innovative and fearless representations of sex and sexuality in First Nations writing and literature.

A few memories stand out; Alison Whittaker's ground-breaking publications *Blakwork* and *Lemons in the Chicken Wire* are both deliciously full of hunger and longing, peppered with cunts, scrags and moots, unafraid of being feral and sensuous at the same time. Ellen Van Neerven presents deeply embodied and high-stakes queer sex scenes in their critically acclaimed three part work of narrative fiction *Heat and Light*. The playfully horny scenes of Melissa Lucashenko's queer protagonist in her Miles Franklin Award winning novel *Too Much Lip* enjoying sex with a cis boy in the shower also come to mind; as do the nostalgic moments of Gary Lonesborough's young protagonist in his much-celebrated young adult novel, *The Boy from the Mish* having his first adolescent gay encounters and heartbreaks on riverbanks and in teenage bedrooms.

Reading each of these works made me want to pinch myself, and it is deeply heartening that our First Nations LGBTQIA+ writers are continuing to boldly assert their right to enjoy and celebrate sex and sexuality in all its complexity and difficulty.

I want to thank all contributors for their thoughtfulness and generosity in sharing these works for Sydney WorldPride and invite readers of all kinds to immerse themselves deeply in these pages.

As you read, you will be struck by the boldness of the writers' audacious self-love, and the deep reverence and restorative love contained within the work for themselves and each other.

Arlie Alizzi

INTRODUCTION

NANGAMAY MANA DJURALI. Dream, gather, grow. This collection was brought together on Dharug Country. Our thanks to Aunty Julie Jones for giving us permission to use these Dharug words.

This collection is a tribute to generations of LGBTQ+ mob dreaming, gathering and growing in our storytelling and in our work subverting words. We dream of another possibility. We gather, build community and family with one another. And we grow until our voices echo over the entire continent.

Some of those rainbow mob whose voices have guided our own are now Ancestors, speaking to us from somewhere else. Some of them are between these pages, voices still calling out or calling out for the first time. As curators of this book, we worked our best to honour them.

What's inside these pages is dear to us. It represents parts of our diverse community — across Nations, genders, ages, class, experiences, places, and poetic forms. It represents every letter in our shared acronym. But these voices have more to tell you than just who they are.

This anthology holds their ambitious poems. They reflect on making memory, on the pleasure and agony of sex, on carceral conditions and violence, on the corporatisation of our communities, on how we find our place among our families, on holding gender in a transphobic colony, on love. And they do it in surprising and exciting ways. These poems have guts and speak directly from them.

Thank you to all the poets in this book, whose work has filled us with pride. To those who read it, we are proud to share it with you.

Alison Whittaker & Steven Lindsay Ross

#mardigrasrainbowdreaming

ʕ⊃❀•‿•❀ʔ⊃ (˅)

the BWS is now a BWyaasssssS as in yass queen as in yasssss gay pride as in yass we stole this lingo from black queer communities on the other side of the world as in BeerWineSpirits is now a place to drink down some black queer liberation on land stolen that locks up blak queer bodies if maybe they've had a bit too much BeerWineSpirits but won't lock up the others who snarl as you walk down the street hand in hand with ya misso on ya way to have a drink

(つ◕‿◕)つ ❤ ≧◉‿◉≦

GayTMs it's like an ATM but it's gayer holds your hand after but doesn't leave a number or maybe moves in on Tuesday or maybe pays for medication yours or nans or someone elses or helps get some kid some mental health care plan to figure out why their body don't seem right but won't grant rights and won't write a cheque and won't write to government about bodies that don't fit between two tick-boxes but will give you the option for a receipt thank you see you next time don't forget your card don't forget your cash don't forget your yasssss queen

≧★‿★≦ (/◕ヮ◕)/*:·゚ ✧

and the google map shows the route in rainbow to the stadium where exec gays and clever rich straights can have front row seats behind the gate to the genuine gays and all those genuine straights who thought it would be so cute to be on the corporate float this year and march alongside the police who would absolutely never systematically target the queer community and who are absolutely not built on a legacy of doing just that and who absolutely don't uphold a colony that enforces an ideology that makes no space for non normative bodies just ask the next lot oh yay it's the liberal party what a special day what a lovely float thanks for spending all that money so everyone could have a vote

(ɔ˘ ³(͡ ‿ ͡c)   ]:->   :^)

instagram is for mardi gras and google is for mardi gras and absolut is for mardi gras and vodafone is for mardi gras and sydney is for mardi gras and mardi gras is for sydney a tourism campaign and mardi gras is for profits for a rainbow banner that holds no one up but gives enough rope to make sure that there is one version of a rainbow and it fits the gaze of execs who had to work hard to be so correct and even went to their cousins wedding two grooms and look this is what the community want and look this is a community with cash and look money is for mardi gras and mardi gras was a protest but protest isn't sexy when it's hard or anti-excess so you can wrap up your bigotry in glitter and call it progress for a weekend and none of these corporations speak up when they come for our rights but hashtag loveislove when everything is over won and done

(/ ● ヮ ●)/ (^o^) (❀ ͡ ‿ ͡ ^)

the blaks get down on a knee and it doesn't make the broadcast and the cops get run out run onto and it doesn't make the broadcast and the community floats get their thirty seconds and the corporate floats get their seventy seconds and the protest before the march is the family event that gets run out run onto by those cops who tried to block the event and on the walk home down oxford street dreaming we get heckled and listen to others screaming and men with iphones ask us to kiss for their private archive and strangers with long range lenses take photos for who knows what archive not asking yass queen mardi gras dreaming sydney wears it's corruptness never fearing and no need to shame your rum colony system feeding rum colony feeding where those who pay get dignity for a day or at least a billboard that is afforded to those who can join and those who can pay thank you thank you sydney for our special diluted day

(͜. ͜) (_!_) (^ ͜^)

Resonance

Trapped by convention
Scared of any attention
Don't wanna be reviled
Life of a closet child
Different from your loved ones
I wore them heavy shoes once
Hearing everything they say
Can turn your day cold grey
They'll make out that it's tragic
But inside you there's magic
And in time you will find
That those like you — they shine
When you see them, you will know
Just how differently they glow
The resonance yet unknown
Will show you're not alone
When your inner spark ignites
You'll glow with your own light
And find that love inside
That they sometimes label 'Pride'

Alita Morgan

Awi sista!

#1

A trans sir see her
She not exotic for youse
She slays for hers lyf

#2

A boy says to Her
image in the mirror She
Is bound to love me.

#3

Me dat boy that was
Born with sugaa in the tank
And swish to slay Yassss

Coming in

In dungarees, in a picture of Dad,
Mum behind the camera
hanging between them
determined, knowing I wasn't me
not knowing it would take too long
Fifty years of this twilight

I hid from worlds not mine,
but was enveloped anyway, and cared for
Black love is like that
Yet I worry, what they'll make of my different body,
my body they didn't expect
It's survivance,
it's knowing we will always be
here

Alex Wilson calls it 'coming in',
to our people
and to love that will be
One thousand years we'll be
here
and forever we have
Yindyamarra Winhanganha
in the body I need
in the body others deserve

Sandy O'Sullivan

Never not thinking (about that)

Queerness does not exempt you from colonial behaviour.
Chelazon Leroux

This is not a dress rehearsal, this is life.
Malcom Cole

Never not thinking about what it means to live in this body
Never not thinking about how uncompromising I am, though so nauseous
Never not thinking about Lidia Thorpe adding colonising to her
parliamentary oath
Never not thinking about the consumptive appropriation of our identities
Never not thinking about what it means to take queerphobia at work
and say *thank you* afterwards
Never not thinking about that doctor, or that hospital, or that room.
Never not thinking about time as an obstacle
Never not thinking about grief as a birthmark
Never not thinking about shame as the engine that drives me away from home
Never not thinking about my best friend who encouraged me to reply:
I define my non-binaryness, not you!

Ellen van Neerven

Ginger

Standing sweat dripping
Redhead raises his arm
Sweet musk

Moon

The thief
left it behind
glowing at the window

my grandmother's two brown hands

i.

night
it always happened at night
the sentimental words we'd exchange with each other
that no one else could hear
that no one was lucky enough to hear fall from your lips
no one – but me
and this night was no different to any other
except for the fact that you –

       glowing in your bardi jawi glory
         and still draped in your gold necklaces
         and argyle diamonds and paspaley pearls

you
were dying
and you knew it and i knew it
but of all the things we spoke about
we never let those words leave the confines of our minds
into the cold darkness of the room
while the moon hung itself in full ceremonial dress in the sky
and peeped through the cracks of the curtains
on your bedroom window

in the silent intervals of our words
i would think of all the things you taught me
and all the treasures you buried into my chest
on our once-in-a-lifetime journey together

Bebe Backhouse

a voyage

that was written for the history books and the movie screens

for everyone to comprehend

but only for us to live

i stared at your soft hair with its burgundy and auburn tints

your stripey nightgown framed you in the body of a prisoner

sentenced to cancer with no eligibility for parole

but certain death row

and i remembered a night

where i'd seen the same moon in the same sky

only shining on you through a different window

as impatient people in souped-up cars

sped up and down russell street

and we

sat

side by side

heart to heart

nan and golden child

ii.

your hands are different now

you said to me

as you fumbled around in your black leather handbag

and balanced a winfield gold between the bounty of your lips

your hands are different now

you must use them to survive – not sweeten

from where we sat on your apartment balcony
i could see the terracotta mask of the world was cracking open
and the slow pace of the birrarung was quickening in its silence
and it was widening between the building that perched us
high above the people on the street
and all the other homecomings of fear

i was everything without you
but when i was with you i was more than this
you were a foreign land that i first remember exploring
in the amazonian gardens of your estate at 375 loch street
you were wonderful and funny
and short-tempered and demanding and elegant
and everything a grandmother should be

i never once wondered why it was me
you gently poured your soft love into
mum would say it was because
i look exactly like my grandfather before he was taken from you
before you were ready to say goodbye

and it's funny
how the design of fate works in repetitive sequencing
because then
it was me who wasn't ready to say goodbye to you

you gifted me with more than your blood and your genes
you gave me a reason to believe in a higher purpose
you held a seat for me at the table in your heart
and you were there for me

you were always there for me
even when i didn't know i needed you
i guess you simply knew

and that night
as the people went crazy ordering chinese takeaway
and watching mindless television
we sat
side by side
heart to heart
grandmother and golden child
and when my heart thumped in its exposed chamber
i leaned into the movements your hands were making

you sipped your cup of coffee and puffed on your cigarette
and flicked the ash onto the tiled terrace
and you combed your hair
in the dread of the little hours of that midnight confessional
and you weaved into the air the message i'd take with me through the
streets of every city i'd
visit
the trees and grasslands and beaches
of the land we knew as home
the horseshoe drive-through of my apprehension
those words –

    use every part of you to carry yourself

and this is —
that was —

how my whole twenty-seven-year-old self
became no more solid than a blade of grass
in front of your brown hands
you —
the woman who once wrestled me — screaming —
into the world of a showery calm
and into my mother's waiting arms

but who
at 7:15pm on the twenty-third of march twenty eighteen
would wrestle me — still screaming —
from your lifeless arms and into safety?
where would my safety be then
when it was always and only with you?

your two brown hands had held me up
more times and more firmly than my own two white feet
but i remembered every part of you
and how you moved
when you spoke to me on top of the world
when you told me my hands were different
and i'd need to use them to survive
not sweeten

and nan
i haven't sweetened
i've cured in the brine of my experiences
and i've become not sour but mature and strong
and i have a taste that leaves a residue

long after i've left the tongue of anyone who bites my spirit
and i've survived

iii.

it's been four years
and i'm still afraid to be distant from you
and what would you say if i told you i'm ready for death?
i don't want to die
but if this is the end then i'm ready for it
because i've lived every day as if they were small existences
and i haven't wasted a single one
and when i go to sleep at night
i close my eyes knowing i've embraced being perfectly imperfect
i let others do as they wish
but i keep breathing the breaths i began thirty-two years ago
and i know that through loving you
and being loved by you
i am strong and i am light
and i am moving boldly through the labyrinth of life

and nan
i am eternal
i learned this
through the intimate interludes between our footsteps
when we shared our heartaches and vulnerabilities
and you gave me reasons to remember and be remembered
and you helped me realise
those very human moments were what made my life so rich

then
and now
and nan
i hope
i hope that you're proud of me as i am of you
and i felt so lucky to know you so deeply
and have your hands —
those soft brown baskets of hope
hold me up
and push me through the darkest of nights

and i hope
when you took your last breath
you thought of how full your life had been

and that in your one final second
you died feeling like the luckiest woman on earth

and nan
the world is crazy
and sometimes people are toxic
and i don't want to be a part of this mess
but i hold my head upright

my head — a crown of thick brown wires
and at the end of each strand
there's a pain
of seeing my home without you in it
but greater than this
there's a love so big and so loud
it declares you essential to me

iv.

i love you
i love you
i need you

i remember you
i remember where we sat
side by side
heart to heart
nan and golden child

and i lift my hands
          again — so different now —
and i take all that you'd made of me
into the ache of this world
and i carry inside me
your blood and your fight and your memory
and your name

roseleen maxine

one sure surviving thing
a part of me
i use
to carry myself

Love & Other Ridiculous Notions of Togetherness

Made in red and born into yellow light that lights up my black skin
Mum fed me her milk while she stayed thin
My black skin is hers and it's where it starts
Mum's love for men leaked into her children's hearts

We walk side by side carrying rainbow flags sweating gold glitter
Foot after foot we march on Stolen Land
We hold hands to make monochrome images and chant in unity
But we are not united

You will go home to your partner and french bulldog
Grateful for everything you have and thank God it's not the 1950's
I will go home and get a notification on my mobile
Jesus Christ, there's been another death in custody

You post a video of you downing a slippery nipple
I post about the fundraiser for the kid's funeral
You cuddle up on the lounge to watch a movie
I'm laying on my bed, looking at the white roof hoping it would collapse
on me

My mum calls me, like she always does after the news
'How are you bub?' She mews
'I'm alright mum.' I implore
As a Black mother, that's all she could ever hope for

I love my mum
I love my people
The homosexuals
The Aboriginals

But it's the type of love that you cover up with a makeup palette
I tap the green into my brown skin
I smile at the mirror
It smiles back

I love you to the stars and back
But you would sell me to Satan for some top rack
I love you like a sinner loves being caught
But you would ruin my body, soul and spirit without a second thought

Three bullets to the chest
He should've worn a bulletproof vest
Gunned down in a club with rainbow lights
By a baldy who hated gays but loved unfair fights

It's 11AM by the chilly pool, thinking about latin pop
You pour a champagne flute to the top
It's 11AM on the cool verandah, thinking about all the wrongs
I crack open a VB listening to sad country songs

I guzzle your cum like it's ichor
You lick my arse with vigour
Our bodies join and I think I love you...
Then you say I resemble a kangaroo

Mum wants me to go to church on Sunday
She hopes she or I can pray the gay away
Mum explains, "Our ancestors were straight as spears."
But she doesn't say shit to Uncle who leers

This is the end, my time is running out
When your finish reading my words I will be dead
Don't cry, don't scream, don't pout
Since the start, there's always been a price on my head

Bubba, You're Gonna Go Home

to the girl who ached for home

who cried

      and cried

           and cried

till there was no ocean left in her

who would dream of salty plum stained fingers

Cradling ice blocks made from cordial

who watched, patiently, as her father dived

and then would join him, mimicking his movements;

limbs blending into sol wata

for the girl who's feet were the colour of dirt

who drowned herself in stories

told under the stars

who wore sunkissed kinks and locks

And always wanted her hair to breathe as much as she did

to the girl with rage in her belly

with anger gripping tight around her ankles

With so much love to give,

even to those undeserving,

hiding behind manipulative eyes

who seek friendship, and relationship to practice power

to abuse, to gaslight, to make themselves feel relevant

A breathing insecurity.

For the girl who will grieve more than she'll laugh
Who will become all too familiar with pain
And loss, as her surroundings become all too foreign
Who will continuously doubt herself beyond reason
Even though she is qualified, and intelligent
And deserving of every joy she manifests
Who will deny herself the right to feel
Invincible
Incredible
Happy.

To the girl with the ocean on her mind
With salt water in her blood
With sand in her hair
With hands that wanted to mend the impossible
With hope, even though she could not find any
Bubba, you're gonna go home

that ache in your chest,
that yearning for the ocean and land that calls you,
will be remedied
because you will return home
you will return to yourself
to your village
to your Dolphin house
with the garden Papa and Nan planted at the front
and you'll sit on the cement stairs
watching the sky melt into the sea
and become infinity
Sis, you will be infinite

Gugurrgaagaa '93
Where a heart like mine belongs

yaraay biri
chorused swirls gala
wrapped myself in you
divided outside, just
conflux scores the tempo

steeped russet skin more strength than
grey eyes, one dark road swoon

'Ain't like I just like I dreamed?'

And we never stay
And you love him
F
   A
     L
       L
EN

Proud in eyes that leap over stuck sorrows
And I did
Kept breath

blinding me with sight that seemed so far
with scar on face kept stubble sharp
frisks more to find you
Yulu-gi wunga-li (danced until you came back)

Colin Kinchela

Easyfree

I don't need you to provide for me
No need to protect and shelter me
I've come this far already
Solo, so far, so high, and so free

I don't need you to impress me
No need to compete
and compare with me
I just need you to be you
(and only you)
Everything you are
Everything you're going to be

Easyfree
Easy and free
No stress, no strain
Free from captivity

Easyfree
free and easy
dont try, dont do
just enjoy, and just be

With Me

I dont need you to puzzle me
No need to question
And decipher me
I just need you to be cool
No obligations
Just respect and honesty

I dont need you to direct me
No need to demand of or order me
just be you, just be cool
relax
Unwind
enjoy the ride with me

Easyfree
Easy and free
No stress, we're blessed
Enjoying sexuality

Easyfree
free and easy
dont try, dont do
just enjoy and be

With Me

Enjoy the time we share
Embrace the space we
create
You and me
Me and you
And the way we relate

Easyfree
Easy and free
No stress, no strain
Embracing spirituality

Easyfree
Free and easy
dont try, dont do
just enjoy and be

With Me

Earth Mother

She lays bare now, since they first arrived here.
All my hurt and my anger just swells as a tear.
It rolls nonstop down my cheek like their bulldozers
through our land.
It's so sacred. She's our Mother, why don't they understand
that every rock and every tree has significance and meaning.
From the very first dawn, the beginning of our Dreaming.
We looked after our Mother, we were keepers of our place.
Slaughtered by the hundreds, we now live in disgrace.
Culled to a minority like cattle at a station,
by Prejudice, Racism and Ignorance of a nation,
So all the mining and all the logging, can't you see, we hear her screaming.
She's screaming to her children, "Please help me keep our Dreaming."
The songs of all our peoples can be heard in our minds,
we get confused living in the city, we could leave them all behind.
So stand up proud and believe and make sure we all help one another.
Don't ever forget where you come from and don't forget your Earthmother.

We stand together

There are many types of lesbian and we don't all get along,

from Dykes to femmes, to celebains.

We know where we belong.

From butches to futches.

From brazilians, to bushes.

Our lipstick lesbians, who always fool the men.

They might look good to them but these ones just want men as friends.

There is closested and pillow princesses and of course our golden stars.

They are the ones who stayed on Venus and never went to Mars.

Some who like to read a book while others drink at bars.

We cannot forget astrological lesbians, who gain wisdom from the stars.

We really have all types,

So don't just generalize.

Some of us like nature hikes, and others prefer motorbikes.

All we ask is just one thing.

To be accepted and to be seen.

For we are just like you.

Loving human beings.

We dream to not be sexualised or criticized

because we step outside the mainstream.

We are a community of creatives, or carers and sometimes terrors.

Our common thread of love is what brings us all together.

We are a species who want to love so let everyone have their dreaming.

Ella Noah Bancroft

future library

I take a seat
to find my place in a story:
how did my body get here?
I cease to remember.

cataloguing warmth
gives me something to do

your constellations
follow me

I reflect
into you

you, my sibling, buried
deep into my chest

and me, a changeling
with

crushed berries
on my dress

your embrace – home-phone
heavy – held tightly my breath

your weight, like
sun's, stretches

my mind
beyond death

sometimes you float to me
in crowds, a single note

on my tongue; a
rose in any context

smells only
like you

things are buried in
my basement, all of them fear

still, you stayed
hidden with me in

our capsule
of rapture

if I fly across the world
do you cease to exist?

my floating mind
not here; my

rotting roots
not there.

I find a seat
and take my place in these stories:
how can your kindness stay here?
I want to remember.

Sea Glass

Down by the water were all the couples, because all the bars on the hill were closed. This side of the river looked towards the sun, so the end of the evenings was magic. Morning twilight is like a good kiss–there without exception, and then gone. While dusk lingers on what's come before, dawn threatens to take the past away.

They had met outside the sealers bar, and outside Michael stayed, with the Blacks, Irish and worst of the drunk children. Michael was drunk too and too drunk to remember Tangana's name. Tangana had known plenty of Michaels, more so in the past year. Michael's excitement was a sort of confidence. To him things felt preordained, like he was his own creator. If he thought something it was true, like the world was changing and he was in it. That was his truth, and the colony's.

Frills and pink satin roughed up on cobblestone under lamp light. Tangana recognised the Irish thieves, caught posing as up-late women. Tangana loved to watch these men's loud behaviour, where laws seemed remade in the damp stone night, but law was the wrong word. This hole in language laughed, calling him in, like an open mouth. The mouth was wide and black.

The further they walked down the hill, the more the rocks gleamed of whale grease. When Tangana caught Michael's loose feet it was the first meeting of their lips, chins, hands, and mouths. It wasn't Michael's first time, but it was his first with a Crow. Still, further to the cove and finally Michael took off his boots. Tangana looked down at the broken glass lodged in Michael's foot. The glass would outlast the evening, smoothed down over years until easily held and collected by tourist hands, no longer sharp or dangerous. The glass was easily mistaken for quartz, a famous feature of the cove. It left everything sparkling at dawn.

Neika Lehman

Suspended Tethering Lives

We're suspended by tethered thread that chain us

to this empire of living ghosts

we're forced to hover above our imminent path into the abyss.

A reality that hits harder than the collision of my tears to the ground,

as another loved ones thread has

been cut

       buckling under the weight.

Time hovering makes you think if there is more feeling other than numb

         because after feeling it all

          to feeling none.

              My dispensary of emotions runs cold.

Because, hello!? Asthma runs in the family.

I choke under the pressure of words that matter

       I choke...

          I choke...

            I choke,

as too does this inheritance of beautifully young lives

filled   with   abundance   of   cousins   play fighting,

which in turn become big rips,   into games of spotlight.

All until the curtains are pulled under you

and you can't remember that last game.

Until the haze blows over and you realise that the abyss has a name

It has an origin

truthfully I'd spend less breath
onto the blame of our mothers and
fathers,

however,

they have been hanging too.

Fat Queer Colony

I occupy too much space.

My sartorial choices are
just as I should.

Options are standard, flagrant designs
to keep my body maligned.

Like cartography, I am
Interpreted and assigned.
Settler colonies remain strict on size.

Sleek and confined
the BMI
Is a symptom of racist quasi science.

A fat queer Aboriginal body
Nothing comes in that phenotype.

Surpassing the gayze
I shed the colonial weight.

I will occupy too much space.

the humble middle ground

the humble middle ground
sits between sovereignty and genocide
it's a place where whites feel comfortable
to engage with the issues
without actually addressing them

the humble middle ground
is a crusade of mass deception
million dollar campaigns
a promise to recognise your voice
that your ancestors gifted you, long ago

the humble middle ground
is injustice disguised as liberation
a thief saying 'wipe your feet
as they invite you through the front door
of your own home

the humble middle ground
will have you settle for their lies
while they continue to settle our lands
a colonial falsehood
commonly known as assimilation

fight for truth
rise up for freedom
settle for sovereignty

Éla

Lick lick
Suck suck
Yassou
I won't cease
You won't stop
You close your eyes
Head chucked back
Oh yassou, yassou
Hello, hello

Lick lick
Blinded by car lights
Strafe me in the moonlight
then plunged into blackness
an engine cut dead
Who that there?
What you want?
Deep and salty,
I know that voice
"Éla."
I know what you want
Gulp your tears of lust

Lick lick
You always remember
Always tender
Even invited me
to your wedding
Oh yassou, yassou

Personless Love

Faceless profiles confess that they find my body desirable.
They say how my skin "glows!"
Indeed it radiates faster than my wit can come to terms with our...
"Meet up"
arrangement.
I'm curious as to where this stranger can lead me through some
curvature of my own body,
I myself do not know the whereabouts to
See in personless love,
it removes the fear of attachment,
because I can't love someone without a heart.
But I can love the person they see me to be
for in that spare moment,
I'm purpose without a journey
Because we've already arrived.
They're finished,
they're done for the night,
until they need their next hit of brief love to sustain themselves,
sustaining by performance,
selling a show abandoned by their bedded truths.
While masquerading their lies that they never loved this body.

Ari Mills

impossible to contain

they said... we are the dust that fine-silts your skin   we are brown
rivers   blue oceans   pink lakes   purple skies   we are fresh water
salted   mined / cracked / drilled   we agitate and distil with mud and
clay   then we rise   awake in the wake   afloat on a legacy that churns
into trouble   and we refuse to be left behind.

they said... we are your constant   we cast shadows and secrets to wax
and wane   caress your face so you glow   we will lure you in and tug
at your heart   we will bathe you   sedate you   shine through night so
you grow toward the sun.

they said... we will surprise you with our velocity   suck the air from
your lungs and whip through your hair so your dark eyes sting   inhale
slowly   with focus   see your flesh tremble   we will teach you to fly
to the stars   this vast complex intricate web of night   there is so
much to say here and we promise to point you home.

they said... bend and glide and carve your way back   this is your journey to
meet the sea   currents will pull you under   for this freshwater spirit
has much to share   you will be gifted gills to breathe in the deep   you
will erode silt barriers   welcome the flow   there will be no
horizons when you arrive   so hold space for the immensity as we siren-
call you   cradle and rock you   we will not let you go.

they said... plant these seeds   grow story-trees with deep roots and life-giving canopies to shelter and nourish and bloom   remember to lean in close   recognise the colour of survival   what it looks / feels / tastes like   we will haunt you and make noise   for the air that you breathe   for clean water you need   for the skin that you bear   for the right to flow free   for the lovers you choose   for love of Country   and do not worry   time can't erode your spirit or your place   know that you belong.

they said... seek us in rainbows and fractures of light   we will find you   drink nectar from your lips and salt from your tongue   introduce you to yesterday's breeze   and soar into tomorrow   everywhere afloat   impossible to contain.

Natalie Harkin

Chocolate

So, you want this piece of chocolate, you
wanna remove it from the shelf

You wanna get high all its sweetness as it
lingers in your mouth

You're addicted to its joyous taste because
never had you felt

The tingle way down of the sweet sugar brown,
yeah, you like how chocolate melts

Well, it's nice you desire such a fine sweet treat
but there's a heat you may feel eating more

So, before you replenish your deep need to fill
a fetish there are things that I'm going to need
assured

Are you ready for a fight when you take a small
bite just to find you're denied what is sweet

Or perhaps you bit too hard on a salty bitter
part as you learn this lovely snack is not all
treat

Steven Oliver

Could you handle the taste that is born of a
place in the waste of compassionless minds

Could you handle me talk of the battles we've
all fought, every time we've had to mind the
cruel unkind

Would you stand in the fire, feel the heat of
our ire that will burn until our hearts know
of peace

Would you try to understand, that this land
upon we stand, has a hurting some seek only
to increase

That our truth is still denied, when you've not
sat with us and cried, when you've not felt the
great injustice that has been

Would you think of it the past, when you've
not felt the way it lasts, you've been gifted
and uplifted from one clean

Come to think of me erratic, brush me off
that I'm dramatic, I'm a fanatic of deep
misery and pain

Deny the hurt that takes its toll on this
hurting weary soul that knows hurt
will come to be felt yet again

Would you find it's not that easy to
believe me yet then tease me with your
words that speak desire in what you say

That once you go black then you never
go back unless black speaks injustice
each day

Would you start to feel frustration and
not like a situation where entitlement
is told it has no place

Where you're made to understand you
won't have the upper hand should one's
hate create debate on state of race

Would you come to waste my time, be
blind to my mind, start to challenge
me with lies instead of fact

Have a fools need to pretend just to
false win in the end, is the integrity of
a man a trait you lack

Then it's best that you replace your
shallow empty chocolate taste if its
flavours are too strong now for your
mouth

If digesting the truth is too painful
with proof as you've only ever been
taught how to doubt

Your stomach weak and queasy now
feeling uneasy for you're thinking
this chocolate's too rich

And you'll only feel better when
you've put back together the image
of a black filthy bitch

If you think this too much, try
living it as such, you may then see I
don't have a choice

You might also then see while desire
runs free never would I give you my
voice

For the love of Crystal

Awiiiiiiiii angila legs, or angila "leg"? (For lols)
Since She da Queen Supreme swallowed a fragment of glass through her
foot. One night,
Breaking up a sistagal fight.

The same gals, mother and a sister. She houses because she is the big
mumma blister ma sister savage as a bitzer. Advocacy. Always fighting
for sistas, Gals. The Sistagals. The brothaboys. She is transient in nature
and transitions between her responsibilities, looking strong but always a
little heartbroken. Celine Dion songs to boot.

But this big boss bitch, forget the tongue biting. Transition lighting.
As she enters, and swallows her people in song. A chosen song she loves
so well it's turned into artistic alchemy. SistaGal of the world.
Crystal Love rising from a Chrisallys.
She will rise, she will rise.

She is Murtangkala, tiwi creation woman,
With the cinema to boot.
The number one toy gal from toy world,
that swallowed a fragment of glass through her foot.

She swallows us like we are water.

My sister like a camp asf Tiddalik the frog.

As she paints her stage and commands our eyeballs, our facial muscles, our heartbeats. She swallows us in her mission to devour our everything for 3 minutes and 48 seconds. She puts da rag in drag and puts crystal diamonds and glitters.

She's an uptown sistagal, my sister. Angila legs, or leg. The leg She is left with after swallowing a fragment of glass through her foot. Gangrene for the Queen Supreme, almost died but lost one leg.

One legend. She swallows entire continents when she travels, the world her stage.

My sister.

Angila legs with one leg gone.

After she swallowed a fragment of glass through her foot.

Freedom?

Jonathon drifts down the hedge
hooded stooped and all
forlorn
but cheerful somehow
youngish and nearly tall
I'm smoking at the front
tossing butts out on
the lawn

he's black
I think
I bet this cunt
bums me for a durry
like a psychic echo
his thick lips mumble
smoke mate?

I wave him through the gate
his approach is shy
and
strangely
overweight
he slowly
tries my
brittle plastic chair
and from mine
I watch

prepare my tin

to open

and through a silver stream of smoke

I get it

later

15 months a lag

15 months no fags

will this new first drag

maybe undo him?

poor kid!

he's lobbed into Wagga

from Lismore

sans tobacco

sans money

sans place

to place his head

alone

his step

uncertain

Yeh

I get it

later

when he's through my gate

parole s'posed to

help

but no go

don't go

no $200

watch you don't go BACK
to jail
for them sad sad sandwiches
fine he'll say
least it's dry
and mates
with words to learn
like
BROTHERS IN ARMS

urge the tin toward him
for four weeks

he cries sometimes
of his Mum
dead when he was leven
gone to heaven
he s'poses
but who knows?
drinks my booze
I choose to let him
smoke more smokes
no joke
to not
smoke
a smoke
a bloke go crazy
which I think he did
long time back

with lack

and

grief

and

hopelessness

Jonathon

snores beside me

three nights like my big

little brother

til

they drop off

from a ute

some mattress

on my front-room floor

with stuff that doesn't fit

sortofsinging

don't ya come back no more

no more

don't ya come come back

no more

with this last advice

and stop ya

trespassing

outside the door of ALDI

that's that sunshine

heard ya livin with

A POOF!

poof yeh

but not wif me

wif me e just UNCLE

e alright

that one blackfella

man

e say I

STAY

long I want to

SO go get fucked

OR I SMASH you GOOD ONE

NAH

no good that one

more jail

MORE fail

then I be 45 neck time

maybe Uncle dead

then

dead then and

then WHAT?

SAMEOLD

Cos he old

Everything I do I do for you

I have indictable charges yet faced
You see I'm in the Walama List
But I don't fear institutions
Irwin's stingray can't even fuck with me
These places are the old shoes
The hole in the toe, the voided place
But if you give me a chance
I can balance on a thread for you
Carrying countless kilos of migaloo law
I have gone around the world in less than a minute
Thank you Grindr explore
Yet when I travelled to you, It felt like home
I've had to find my way through a thousand mazes and still I'm never lost
For I know to find, is to not know
This isn't the ending
I can breathe in and out of water
A contemporary precursor of the didgeridoo
I would travel to the end of the volcano for you simply because
I lava you
I taste the scorn like bullets
and the buds of my tongue tingle and
My creativity flies like butterflies
Reborn like a caterpillar
You see
I can build a brain like they do a bear without even reading the instructions
I can speak all the languages of all the alphabets and my ancestors before me
I have more of a vocabulary than any dictionary

and more meaning than any thesaurus

My DNA is one of the oldest

I have the sight of an eagle,

the nose of a dingo

The tough skin of a bony brim fish

I can walk barefoot on iron nails

I am immune to death

I don't need blessings because I always have good luck

Come with me for a walk

Because I have more stories to tell you than García Marquez

Look

I always was a daydreamer

Rustling leaves and shifting loose rocks

Mindlessly exploring, mindfully present.

I daydream of love

The kind that is uncompromising

Unconditional

For you, everything I do, I do for you

You get the best of me

For I am everything that I am

Because you are everything that I need

I am your greatest dream

And your worst nightmare

I see in the dark without using a flashlight

I cook what you want as I am a lover of food

I can blow the grey clouds away so that you have a good day

For you, I cross borders without a visa

And I give you the good smile that is missing on the Mona Lisa

For you, I breathe before I die

For you I go to church and listen to the entire mass without falling asleep

You see

I dance across meadows that aren't even mine

The more that time goes by, I feel younger

I hold that child, the one that is me

And I wrote this poem without even listening to Beethoven

I hear the birds chirping their daily sounds

A language of love and mystery

Moving wistfully from branch to post

They fly to the whoosh of freedom

Imprisoned by nobody

As the crow crys a shrilled call

Speaking an unspoken language to human ears yet

Announcing to me - you are alive

For you, everything I do, I do for you

So that you get the best of me

I am everything that I am

Because you are everything that I need.

They say black lives matter, mine does and so does yours.

I have power in me, this is the truth and baby, I fucking shine.

choreography

i walk to the sound
 of creased curtains rustling against an open window
 of nature cunningly finding people's weakest spots
 of friends arriving on doorsteps with flowers and boardgames
 of thinking there is more than one life to live
 of pedestal fans humming on still nights
 of outcasts tracing their shadows against brick walls
 of finding faith in what can never be held

i dance to the song
 of compassionate and wide morality
 of skipping down cobblestones on muggy afternoons
 of mechanical hands ticking in clocks on dining room walls
 of lovers unwrapping porcelain gifts on birthdays
 of children living each day as separate little adventures
 of bearing unjustified loads to warrant existence
 of currents of obsession and fear

i make love to the beat

  of glass doors sliding wide open

  of fingernails impatiently tapping on restaurant tables

  of psychotherapy entwined in general conversation

  of hands scarcely touching on forked roads

  of brown birkenstocks on hardwood floors

  of smoking in parks with dizzy heads

  of emotions shifting internally

i live to the rhythm

  of mothers speaking their baby's names for the first time

  of clean white sheets air drying in sunlight

  of the oppression of the patriarchy

  of veils uncovering languages spoken by broken hearts

  of self-sacrificing naivety

  of leaning on balustrades overlooking oceans

  of learning to love deep and dark insecurities on lonely nights

Dangalaba soul water

Feet slipping on purple ochre
The soft flow of bunimudla
Receiving rain
As your Country's daughter

I see the freedom of Queerness
In the ever shifting sunset
That accepts the sun's continual movements
And gifts the world an evolving portrait
Of colour
And hues
A skyline that smiles back at you
And says 'aren't we both just so beautiful?'
And we just big smile back 'ayyyyy true!'

Country gifts us variation
And space to be unique
Like that bird that flies over head
Or that shell that washes up at your feet
It says wouldn't it be beautiful
To create something new?
Forms a new inlet to the river
New gum leaf colours
And then spends some time
Creating you

I find myself in running water
In wide open, shade giving leaves
I find peace in moss covered mud
With mangrove roots digging deep
This is where I find my Queerness
In the weaving of the pandanas leaf
In the large eyed children
Arms reaching up
Asking for their Aunty

This is where I am
Where I have always needed to be
Everything that I need is here
In this land, in this sky, in me

March with Pride

To be Queer
Is to be in step with your ever-shifting spirit
Even when your spirit
Is out of step with your surroundings
Today, I am who I am

To be Queer does sometimes mean
To sit in awkward silences with family
Or to block punches as you walk down the street
To not be able to read about people like you in books
To have your morality talked about on tv
To be told who you are is a phase
And that no one else in your family's gay
(Although we suspect otherwise, eyebrows raised)

To be Queer
Is to be in sync with the rhythm of life
Pounding the ground on arrival
I am here
I am Queer
I am flying through the air
Like a brick to the face of the colonial state
The first Pride March was in rage
Led by black and brown Trans women
It grew to a global movement
That couldn't be contained
The first Pride March

Was a protest
As colonial laws tried to force us into corners
Tried to force us to dark places in our minds
They said conform to these binaries
We said it's not within our nature
To be straight lines

But over the years
We've been sold conformity
For corporate promotion
And capitalist greed
The pink dollar in exchange for a token show on tv
If we shave away enough of our edges
We could fit more snuggly into heteronormativity
Pride March has become powered by banks and capitalist values
Cops are invited to march alongside the same people that they persecute
Being a cop is not an identity
It's an armed and violent branch of the ongoing colony
An institution designed to maintain systems of control
And to protect private property
The police don't give a fuck about your safety
If the laws changed tomorrow
They would enforce without hesitancy
The police is not an identity

The same people who created laws to confine us to closets
Now play inception and confine us from the inside
What does it mean now to march with Pride?
To march in straight lines

Eyes fixed on a projected concept of freedom
That does not stop to pause at the intersections
Who else in this world sits at the intersection of gay
And who isn't marching today
Not out of lack of pride or out of shame
But because we're still raging at the many injustices performed by the state
And white cis gay culture seems to think that that's ok
Then goes on to appropriate the language, culture and dress
Of black and brown finesse
Regurgitates to make money
Without working to make amends
There's a reason that black and brown had to be added to the flag
Cause we're still fighting for the same visibility
As back in 1970
And it seems to me
Pride March chose assimilation
Over solidarity

Not everything that glitters is gold

So today we chose safety over visibility
And not from outside, but within our own community
Rainbows and loud music just isn't enough
And we've come to realise
You were never really marching for us

Colonial fetish— Part 1

Spit.
Hood.
Cuffs.
You
resist.
Hand
on eyes,
your left enduring.
Exerted breath.
Silence
from the line.
The beat,
desultory,
ceasing.
Stained
white
linen.
Frankincense oil.
CCTV.
No remorse.
Praying.
Preying.
Thirst
to kill.
Their thrill.
Sink now
into
paradise.

Pain

we people who have walked in darkness
have seen a great light
it is the delight of pain
but
but
but
the instinct is
avoiding pain and clichés like the plague
like pain
not knowing how
in voiding shit
begets the greatest joy
Indeed
the yanks enshrined it
we have the right to pursue happiness
but for myself there are times
when I like pain
love pain
seek pain
indeed like booze
often reek of pain
because the gain from a straining cock
up my anus
strangely gives both
please and pain
redolent of janus
facing both ways

John Mukky Burke

sometimes looking back
depending on the bloke
whose tack is now to give
and then to spread his poke offering
and strain and cry with my meagre
offering
for his nightly fix
for he too likes
the feel of dicks
with pain
in pianola palaces of pleasures
sometimes fannies
where the straight ones
all in self denial
rely on aching cunts
to satisfy and relieve both their pains
and yet
and yet
and yet
the paradox
remains

pain
is mostly missed
deliberately
if we can help it
just as a sunflower

turns towards its source
and of course
a tiny bub must
relieve its course of pain
in the normal run of
growing
going now
and going then
towards the flowing tit
it proceeds
from the pain of his arrival
indeed
his true survival
makes it thus
and the big plus
life
continues life
with all its strife
and dread and
will go on until
he's dead
and let's hope it was mostly
pleasing
because leaving sans
a sense of satisfaction

is so

how can I say?

disappointing

and makes no sense

hence embrace the pain

that is our life

as we know it now

and yet

and yet

and yet

is there yet a heaven

where surfers

construction workers

cowboys and muscle boys

all smoking

are freely free

for you and me

in some other heaven

with only joy

no pain?

How we die
(for David Hardy)

We die with dignity
I've never witnessed
Pain like that
Pain you couldn't endure
that took everything
Yet you worried about
how I'll be, how old me will live without older you
the pain I feel isn't real

You died of hunger and you drowned
They're the things you controlled that
we couldn't change
In the days before, you told the nurse 'They, not she'
My hero advocate
you laughed when the doctor asked if I was your wife
'I'm gay', you said,
'my sibling',
'your sister,
'my sibling', you insisted
They didn't get it
and you drew a line under it
They didn't really matter

When I think of warriors, I think of you
there with ancestors now
you fought and gave up so much for others
Your beautiful queerness there in love, always

You brought the blanket that the Aboriginal liaison officer in Canberra
gave you
they ordered you barramundi and got you talking about things that
matter
You were angry
sad
determined
a lifetime of caring for others
then you died and I found the poems you wrote
the pain you felt from losing Mum
our tether

I read them to see the pain before the Pain
now what I also feel is Pain
That could have been
a command and goodbye
But you had last minute directions for us
cake at a wake and a fund for older queer Mob
Because, of course

I know how we die

she's gone and near

she's gone and near

In the moment
when I wake I see
my Mum and she is waving
and she's gone

On a walk
It's early, still the river
heart beating soft,
it breaks again
again

One time I've just hopped in the car
Thinking of how she'll look
And what she'll say
And whether her night has been okay
And then I remember
I remember, and it hurts

A Grass Tree by Any Other Name

Flora and fauna have taken over the apartment.

We come together spreading like wild fire, like rain.

Not the country we had hoped–three flights high

On stolen land–but it's our slow-growing peace

For when we tire of the Australian Dreamtime.

A place we can hang our emu feather earrings,

Wash ochres from each other's skin, leave our keys

In a coolamon carved from the knee of a river red,

Without white superstition or political subtext.

Spectacles recede into the chirping suburban buzz

And flushed by an ancient patience, green thumb,

I watch your hedge magic season our landscape

In wetness opalescent as crocodile tears. Almost

Lyrical the way you spin leaf and afternoon light.

A ceremony taking your time tending the grass

Tree, potted knee-high, stump burnt black, stem

Sun-soaked and sprouting past our heads. Flowering

names we keep a secret. This bush love sacred.

Luke Patterson

Dream

I dream about happy Black babies
I dream about loud corroborees
I dream about walking barefoot through the bush
I dream about big fires with people all around

I dream about her hand in mine
I dream about butterfly kisses
I dream about his chest against mine
I dream about sleepy laughter

I dream about the koalas sleeping in the eucalyptus trees
I dream about kangaroos bouncing across the hills
I dream about platypuses creating the rivers
I dream about emus laying eggs across the skies

I dream about gardens of lilli pillis and yams
I dream about a stone and paperbark cottage
I dream about stone fish traps
I dream about woven lomandra bags

I dream about not convincing Settlers of my Ancestors' humanity
I dream about not being institutionalised
I dream about not being neglected in a hospital bed
I dream about not being chained up by metal cuffs

I dream about treaty
I dream about nationhood
I dream about freedom
I dream about a new age

I dream about then
I dream about now
I dream about soon
I dream about ...

My awakening eyes

My awakening eyes
The mirror demands me
A ghost gazes back
How silly are these walls
Languages of the oppression
Tears begin to fall
You see
As the lock clicks shut
I realise this is home
A place society has forgotten about
Where folks in green are alone
They say governments create ghettos
Hoods of concrete and steel
Where unhoused folk come
For that warm 3 o'clock meal
I wonder what caged the bird
For they can no longer sing
As trees constantly fall
To these jungles of steel
Slavery of sorts
Watego reminds us
The colony continues
Their beds continue burning
You try to break free
I can't breathe and you suffocate
The cycle repeats
If walls could only talk

I know the ceilings would cry

The floors shed blood, you see

This is a place where the already broken go to die

The judge can only act on what the police can find

But you can only imprison my body

You'll never pollute my mind

Free everything they say

That's all you black cunts are after

At night when I lay in bed

I can feel their pain, you can hear their laughter

Lost lives to this system

They gone way too young

I hope to see you again my budda

When my body gives out

When I see my final sun

Until that day comes

I'll cry for you once more

I will continue to speak your name

I'll knock on every door

So I write

Dear black

A connection to my soul

Fly high in the sky

Too far to see

Too close I feel

Leaving for the dreaming

I hear you once more

They can't say your name

As blood stains their floor

redbellyblacksnake

the first time I knew
I would hold you always
a mother
      red belly black snake
glided by
as we loved
underneath the eyes of the Illawarra
      blessing us
she was all fertility and love and safety

      the birds knew us
in the old languages
saw the love we were going to grow
      I collected
little branches from above our heads
a token of a sacred place
      it felt like
we were returning and being returned
to the land

that two women have laid together
under these trees
      always
and we were welcome once again

Stick together

White meat pinching
The nose like two ibis
Meet again, not ready to forgive
Packed into the neck like a
Throat packed beneath the crust of the
Earth forgiven, forgiveness like a secret
Birthday cake, now rots in the
Creamy wetlands, clay bitten like cake
All over by birds and bird feet circling
A nucleus of crickets still
Damp, only some can stay still when damp &
Cold growing when we forget to
Reconcile & with spinal force & straightening
Sorry in the eyes like lipstick
They say the ibis circle desperate bodies
& the kiss of unwashed clothes
& the beastly twitching nucleus of good friends
Good queer molten core
Ritual of eyes packing up the face to reconcile
Ask for me $ ask for me
Won't turn away
Not for money & glut
Not for health or safety

I touch the wound and it doesn't hurt as much as the first time

You state your needs so easily.
I never offer mine.
You live out your passions.
I merely follow along.
You indulge yourself in courage.
I am sitting in discomfort.
I want to keep restraining myself
I want to tie myself up in a web
I want to keep myself safe
I don't want to hold me
I want to keep me held down
I want to keep my head down
I want to be seen
I long to love her,
my messy crying self,
or at least know her.
Be with her.
Don't run from her.
Be near to her,
messy crying girl.
I want to ask her:
what would you want if there was no risk?
would your answer be different if fear was removed?
I need freedom.
I am turned on by freedom.

I desire self-direction of time, path, and being.

The root of depression is fear,

the dampening of my life-force.

My happiest moments are with me,

when I am free to be me.

Is that selfish?

I am independent and solitary;

I desire deep love and passion.

I need freedom to feel.

I refuse to be afraid of my heart.

Rage is my life-force.

Care is my life-force.

They want to be seen.

I touch the wound and it doesn't hurt as much as I thought it would.

You can't pray the Gay out of me

The nuns pray for brotha boy
bless his path with golden light

so he visits each day on his way home

he glimmers
everywhere he goes

true gawd

my girlfriend and I sneak kisses between the
clothing racks in the
opp shop

so they pray for us too

hands clasped together at the chest in

like anjali mudra no ahimsa

with hopes we find the lord
and the light and
heteronormativity.

Queer shame doesn't glimmer

so I wear glitter to hide it

find rainbow sequins
on sale

I smile and thank the Sister

as we leave Grandfather Sun
gives a blessing of his own
and with it

I shimmer
everywhere I go.

un_domesticated

Growing up all I ever really wanted in life was to
be one of the following three characters – if not all
of them...
super woman

      spider woman

            bat woman

I could never aspire to becoming a "cat-woman"
as I was self-warehoused into a fear so deep,
so neurotically entrenched among any members
originating from the felidae family tree.
I feared the humble domestic moggy for as far
back as my memory elasticated.
So dire, so drastic, so real was my scaredy-cat fear
of the feline shadows it actually left me in a true
state of pussy paralysis, until, at the very least,
my late twenty-somethings.
But that's another apologue – for another page perhaps?
Rewind to 1983, entering high-school. I pleaded with
my parents to let me opt out of the home-economics
subject in lieu of *Biology One-on-One the Basics*.
For I had already softened to the home-economics
teacher from an angled distance across the netball courts
and in my curious worldview that could only mean one thing.
Intuitively she made me feel sensational in places where
I didn't know one could feel sensational. Thus began my
obsessive compulsive disorder toward long-legged vintage
women of the super-heroine persuasion. I knew in my

Yvette Henry Holt

heart of hearts that this desire of lust would eventually spell disaster for many episodes yet to come.

For she was my super spider bat all rolled into the one DC extravaganza.

First day of enrolment and there she stood triumphantly in front of the blackboard with razzamatazz legs, free-flowing hair akin to the dairy hues of homogenised egg-nog, calling the morning class-roll with a click of her provincial Dutch native tongue.

She was the Bo Derek of kitchen hardware in a tight fitting pair of clogs with thick pillowy lips, the same lips that ran over my every vowel and syllable with words I struggled to pronounce such as stroopwafe, poffertjes, pannenkoeken and kibbeling.

Indeed, Ms Meijer, affectionately known as Ms May, certainly left me irriguous and I don't mean pumpkin scone moist either. I'm talking serious infringement of sexual identity, hidden desires, confusion of self, embarrassment, wonting of scent, improper imaginings. It soon became impossible to separate the fantasy from the reality.

Consequently my parents did not succumb to the pleas of switching me over from home-economics to biology. I was driving my parents crazy and I knew it. All vital signs of domestic input on the family home-front went out the window the moment I started dreaming of windmills and red tulips.

Washing up — I wasn't interested.

Making the bed — never heard of it.

Bringing in the washing on laundry days – impossible.

I sweated out the first term like a crustless wholemeal
cucumber sandwich left all alone on the acacia-wooden
bread-board waiting to be either consumed or discarded.

I soon began to enjoy the weekly visual toing and froing
stares between Ms May and I, as we lowered our
extending fingertips into a myriad of Tupperware bowls,
kneading and Rolfing exotic pantry substances such as
flour, sugar, oatmeal, milk and eggs.

Butter was optional.

According to the then legendary teenage girl bible
magazine – Dolly, the last thing I needed was to
harbour a bleeding internal crush on any teacher.

I was roller-skating on thin ice and I knew it.

Shame on her for making me feel so lost inside
my own pre-pubescent skin.

By the time final terms saddled up, suddenly it
dawned on me that I would never morph into a
bat woman, a spider woman or a super woman.

I had to face facts – I willed myself to put all Mattel
dolls aside once and for all.

Eventually I outgrew my high-octane penchant for
the Saturday morning cartoon re-runs too. I had to let
sleeping DC heroines lay, preferably in the backyard
cemetery next to the laid to rest budgerigar and a

junkyard full of Match-Box cars.

Fast forward to a brand new millennium and I can
now concur that in the long run I never did fair too
well in the domestic goddess Olympiads. I could
never conform to the wrapped-up butterfly motif
apron strings stainless steel state of wellbeing.

Nor did I ever master the artful skill of sharpening
Japanese kitchen knives in preparedness for Sunday
roasts.

I did however surpass the necessary grade for theory
and practicality of home-economics without too much
self-inflicted emotional injury. In fact I had heard
along the passionfruit vine that my take-home
lentil-walnut energy bars were a backyard hit among
the chorus line of neighbouring Garfields. That alone
made me feel proud.

Crikey, the world was still thawing out from the Cold
War

and my biggest dilemma had been to pontificate over an
entire school year between my dearly beloved Maggie
May

versus warm apple pie.

The clouds lifted, the shackles broke and I was no longer
compelled to the infantilisation of comic book charac-
ters

propping up my self-worth of who I was and all I had yet
to become.

I joyfully made global peace with neighbourly kitty-cats
the world over.
And I certainly didn't need the excess crushing of
a teenage heartache to nurse for decades to come either.
By the time I saluted a farewell to arms of
home-economics, Thatcherism was well and
truly in full-swing and every now and then Ms May
would ladle a quote upon unquote of the Iron Butterfly herself:
Any woman who understands the problems of running
a home will be nearer to understanding the problems
of running a country.
Neoliberalism at its finest, perhaps?
Un_domesticated in *home-economics*, overthrown!

The Quiet Work

you soften me
like butter and onions
and it is hard to do the right thing
to love without sacrificing a piece of me

I remember your palm
outstretched and warm
while I wept
that was long ago

gently and firmly, I told you
I will always be on the other end
it is there I will have to be
not here

I think I am going to do
the quiet work
of loving myself
before it is too late

Palangalite

The forest of deep time
Unravelling and unfurling
From its wooded tangled threads, binding
Its arms tied behind its back and to its feet
Escaping the vice like grip and only to be captured
Millennia after Millennia
Creaking and aching
Soothed and summonsed only by the song
And dance of the witch doctors
Pushing their hardened feet and toes
Through the warm red sand,
Heated by the sun and by the friction of black skin
And the constant breath of the song and the word
Countless tongues singing and speaking the songs of the Mother

This is their domain
In the blinding light of the star
And under the twinkling light of the infinites
With its dark water holes and deep swirling pools
Pirnang nyawi, partikalang nyawi
Over and over, rolling and folding forever
It is in the pulsing of their hearts
Pushing the blood through their veins
To their fingers and toes and into their eyes
Seeing, surveying and stewarding Country
Knowing her movements and delicate moods
As she shifts, they shift

Perched, tense they unleash
A song and a dance for every subtle imperceivable nudge

Every cycle is a world within a world
Concentric circles sweeping over and into each other
They only know by moving with her, dancing
Across the fabric of the Yemurraki
Flowing with her, across the plains and under the river
Her siren songs are messages to gather
And to echo her call, honouring the sine
The banging of branches of the puletch
Is the rhythm of the clap stick
Breaking through space, ricocheting and echoing
The cold marrik marrik rustling the leaves
Is the whirring bullroarer
Calling the sweaty black bodies for the waripa
The endless dance to honour her.

They come and gather in the red sand clearing
Brushed and adorned with her jewels
From deep within her womb
Pulled sticky flesh, yawirr
And wawurr from her songbirds
Harkened by Country
The witch doctors take her songs
And spin them through the earth and dust
In a frenzy of sweaty limbs

Dripping and spent, they lay mangled and entwined
Bound to each other without form
Mud and bone clung together
Emulsified and indistinguishable
From the sky, body and earth below.

Pieman Heads

I try not to bring impressions with me
as we step from the boat
the 'SHE', Miss Arcadia II
connects us with new journeys
even if our touching
irked the helmsman

pissed up over the sand dunes
among skeletons still standing
and countless pairs of feet
Djon said this continent's
first portraits were marked in sand
used to tell community by their soles

breakers quaked like an old TV
the spray was waking me up
at the end of the bar I   spear-kissed you hard
wondering again if i'm too much
do you think all my self-evidence in landscape
is a bit of a bore? My instructions to look at this stick?

Here could be the final outpost of the world
where infinity or futures come to die
the government's need for nuclear narcissism
'old friends' shaking hands with turned backs
Marsden taught us threat in all the wrong people
would he approve of making love here?

Fam is Blak

The stench of bleach
marched down corridors
two by two.

                Black bodies hunched forward
                in shadows
                6 to a cell,
                a meat-works.

                        And while forbidden to engage
                        I stopped for a moment
                        to acknowledge,
                        Them.

One would be remiss to think
he was alone
in this crime scene.

                While the 14
                and more
                gathered to do their business,
                those locked away
                would blame themselves.

                        And I know this
                        because I blamed myself,
                        like the Black man
                        who shared his cell.
                        Whose fist

staunchly raised in court
to our family
as he wept
asking our forgiveness.
I get it.

My pillow molded from tears

My pillow moulded from tears
into the shape of 'I could not save him'.
into the shape of 'Not my kin'.
into the shape of 'No justice, no peace',
and,
'Stop Aboriginal deaths in custody'.

Bleach.

Have you smelt yourself lately?
Rung out your mop lately?
Coronially-infested yourself
into the hood
from where you torture souls
and attempt to asphyxiate
the most beautiful
creation that ever was.

While the dream you dreamed for him
rendered him to a dark place
with desultory beat
half-hearted.
It was here where we met once more.
Dreaming.

In visions
while he dances with creation
your prison songs silenced
as country sings back
to remind you that
'You have no place here'.

Bleach.
If the only thing you think connects us
is that you were there
in that moment
baring witness to our grief
hearing our cries
seeing our humanity
seeing how we resisted
well...
You would have neglected to recall
that they were there too.
500 and thousands more.

They were always here.

Generations before your conception.

Thousands of years.

Bleach.

You can not bleach Blak.

You can not wipe away, wipe out, white out,

Blak.

Bleach,

you can not bleach Blak.

Carp

Fat carp smack up
our boat. Far up,
far out, flap out
the tarp. The sad
thing sags — a barb.
A barb.

A Barbara at Coonabarabran
eyes our jackets and
my pierced nose. But
she gives us coffee
to be scrambling up
the escarpment to park
our car. Put a
fist in my hair
while I feast.

What strange love have
you brought me, gub
carp from the city?
If we were fish,
like we are almost
now, parsing east the
river veins. And say
a Barbara, a pest
a barb like a

*We are afflicted with
these disgusting,
mud-sucking
creatures—bottom
dwelling, mud
sucking creatures.*

*The only form of
control is a version of
herpes; it is the only
thing that will get rid
of these disgusting,
mud-sucking
creatures. We will
move forward on this
because we believe*

*that we should be
getting rid of these
disgusting, mud
sucking creatures in
order to support
some of the better
animals of our
waterways—the
silver perch, the*

carp, pulled you up
far up her boat.

yellowbelly, the
Murray cod, the

I don't want to think about it.

You'd flop on a
hot tinny floor you
fellow, with your lot.
Gut both you gubs
so you don't pop.

Eastern cod and the
catfish. You have to
go to some extreme
measures at times to
make sure that we

The Fisheries Management Act
encourages, but does not mandate, such
things.

And then hello, yellowbelly
bedfellow. Bellow gasping. Fold
like this foil on the
fire — lips together to
vent, I think, and
lips and lives together
for Centrelink.

keep our economy
and our environment
healthy—even if it
requires a version of
a venereal disease to
deal with the carp. If
that is what is

If we were fish,
like we are eating
now, yellowbelly sweeping in
from the west. Then
idly resting your breast,

required, then that is
what is required.
We...are going to
make sure that we
have healthy rivers

knowing what love we
know to detest. A
proselyting tide spreading up
the highways

and a healthy
economy, because we
are going to get rid of
the carp.

The carp didn't start this. This is my ways.

— Barnaby Joyce
May 2016

Sacredness Sewn of Footprints

I feel black joy beat from the masses of these lands.

The rivers of energy flowing through bodies, breath, veins, and flesh.

Breathing an observation; winds of wisdom lay my attention.

Swarming me a warmth, a proud joyousness of blackness.

Kneeling to roots, ancientness connects me.

History embedded from the fingertips; footprints lay before me shake a spark of survival.

Ancestors shift solidness beneath my stand, peering through a chiselled sky from my hand.

Faces unblemished outlined of black fineness, I shed my westernised falseness and lay naked of life.

Sacredness sewn of footprints intertwining of veins tying country to flesh and blood to water.

Caught by whispers upon the breathing glands, these lands still sing.

The mind minimising to rest, my words vanish as I wake a gasp of the reborn.

Sacredness sewn of footprints; I follow.

THE POETS

Bebe Backhouse

A descendant of the Bardi Jawi people of the Kimberley region of north-Western Australia, Bebe Backhouse is a writer and artistic leader who's called Naarm (Melbourne) home for ten years. Beginning his creative practice as a classical pianist and composer, Bebe later made a name for himself as a producer and director of theatre, festivals, and public art projects across Australia, including international dance and theatre projects in New Zealand, France and Belgium. Holding senior leadership positions at prolific organisations across Naarm, Bebe has successfully fostered many creative opportunities for Aboriginal and Torres Strait Islander creatives to showcase their work in mainstream platforms, allowing Traditional Culture to thrive in the public realm.

A leader in designing and delivering high-profile programs and strategic projects for Australia's diverse communities, Bebe is a published author and a frequent commentator on the arts and culture community. Holding cultural integrity at the forefront, he has in-depth experience in stakeholder management and is a strong organisational executive leader, with a passion for advocacy, advancement, and the health and wellbeing of Aboriginal and Torres Strait Islander people.

Ella Noah Bancroft

Ella Noah Bancroft is a proud Bundjalung woman currently living and working on Country.

She is a descendant of the Bundjalung peoples of northern New South Wales, and also has blood lines to Scotland and England. She is a Connection coach, writer, poet, mentor, activist and creative, and also carbon neutral event co-ordinator. She is the founder of the Yhi Collective. Ella Noah Bancroft is an active advocate for The Decolonisation movement.

She is passionate about re-wilding the world and the feminine force. Through her writing and work Ella has been promoting re-wilding, the return of the black matriarchy, and decolonising of personal, social and ecological wellbeing for 10 years. She is widely respected amongst her community and believes in local communities with local economies as a way to find hope for the health of our planet and people.

Ella is the founder and director of The Returning, a Not-for-Profit event that takes place just outside of Byron Bay, Australia. The Returning provides a place for all women from all walks of life, to come together to relearn the way of their past, to connect to herbalism, activism, motherhood, health, movement and deep connection to the land She is currently on the board for Women Up North. Women Up North is a northern New South Wales service for women, children and young people who have experienced domestic or family violence or abuse.

Samuel Barsah

Samuel Barsah was born in Townsville, Queensland; his father is from Murray Island in the Torres Strait and his mother is of Aboriginal and Torres Strait descent from Cloncurry, Queensland. Sam started his education at the Black Community School in Townsville with Uncle Eddie Koiki Mabo and completed high school in Ballina, New South Wales. At 17 he came to Sydney and auditioned for NAISDA (AIDT). While at the Dance School he discovered his voice for singing and passion for writing.

John Mukky Burke

John Albert Burke appropriated the name Muk Muk and Mukky after University of Queensland Press asked in 1993 if he had a Koori name that could go on the cover of his David Unaipon award novel *Bridge of Triangles*. Likewise, he used this name on his RADA Award-winning *Night Song and other Poems* in 1999. This, like his gradual acceptance and adoption of his sexuality has, and still does inform his being comfortable with the person he has always been: the social construction of human identity arguably begins the moment our parents choose our names for us.

Mostly we don't question this. Now he is proud of having played a role in taking control of himself. This has been greatly aided by inestimably important projects such as the one that led to this book.

He received all of his schooling in Wagga Wagga in the 50s and 60s, a period of history when the received wisdom was that this racist/homophobic city in a very white Australia (recall the white Australia policy was in odious full swing), had NO Aboriginal people there and certainly no HOMOSEXUALS. Being a fearful but obedient little Aussie, he eventually married and fathered two fabulous kids. In time he greeted three wonderful granddaughters and has a much happier life than in his youth. He turns 77 in 2023.

Andrew Farrell

Andrew Farrell is a Wodi Wodi person and Queer identified academic whose research is focused on LGBTQIA+ Aboriginal peoples and social media. Andrew has also developed projects such as the Archiving the Aboriginal Rainbow blog, an online portal that addresses the absence of a digital space that catalogues Aboriginal and Torres Strait Islander sexual and gender diversity by sharing links to contemporary and historical audio, images, articles, art, and various other items found across the web (Farrell, 2014). The blog prioritises the perspectives of Indigenous LGBTQIA+ peoples as decolonising agents within Nakata's (2007, in Farrell, 2015) 'Cultural Interface'—in which Indigenous LGBTQIA+ knowledge, experiences, and challenges filter through complex terrains of knowing and unknowing—transforming how we may see and know this unique and diverse community.

Dominic Guerrera

Dominic Guerrera is a Ngarrindjeri, Kaurna and Italian person, residing on Kaurna Yarta. Dominic is a poet, art producer, writer, art curator and likes to dabble in photography and pottery. After working 18 years in Aboriginal Community Controlled Health, Dominic switched gears and moved to the arts sector and has been learning their skills as a producer, programmer and curator. Dominic's written work has been published in *Granta*, *Fine Print*, Artlink and *IndigenousX*. In 2021 Dominic was the recipient of the Oodgeroo Noonuccal

Poetry Prize for his poem, 'Unwelcome to Country'. Dominic spends his private time gardening and playing with his pet, Sugar the Chihuahua.

Dr David Hardy

Dr David Hardy was a gay Wiradjuri man who devoted his time to caring for others, including his Mum in the last few years of both their lives. David had a career as a diplomat overseas, he worked as a commissioner with Trade Queensland, and as a member and president of the Brisbane Pride Choir. Throughout his work he always supported others and privileged the work of First Nations writers and artists. He was the first man to graduate with a PhD in Indigenous Knowledges (Creative Writing) from Batchelor Institute of Indigenous Tertiary Education, where he worked editing a revival of the *Ngoonjook* journal, and as a research fellow until his death,. David's creative writing PhD focused on what it is to be a queer, Aboriginal man on a journey of discovery. He used this work, along with his emerging understanding of the aged care sector, to develop a book called *Bold: Stories from Older Lesbian, Gay, Bisexual, Transgender and Intersex People*. David died in May of 2022 following a short, fierce battle with lymphoma. Knowing he was about to die, he worked with the Centre for Global Indigenous Futures to set up a research fund (Dignity) to develop advocacy tools for older queer Mob.

Natalie Harkin

Natalie Harkin is a Narungga woman and activist-poet living on Kaurna Yarta, South Australia. She is a Senior Research Fellow at Flinders University with an interest in decolonising state archives, currently engaging archival-poetic methods to research and document Aboriginal women's domestic service and labour histories in South Australia. Her words have been installed and projected in exhibitions comprising text-object-video projection, including creative-arts research collaboration with the Unbound Collective. She has published widely, and her poetry includes *Dirty Words* with Cordite Books in 2015, and *Archival-poetics* with Vagabond Press in 2019.

Yvette Henry Holt

Yvette Henry Holt heralds from the Bidjara | Íman-Yiman | Wakaman Nations of Queensland – a multi-award-winning poet, her works have been published and translated in multiple languages online and in print for more than two decades. Yvette is the Executive Chairperson to the First Nations Australia Writers Network (FNAWN), and Board Director to Australian Poetry (AP). Since 2009 Yvette has lived and worked upon the unceded lands of the Central Arrernte peoples where she delights within the tiled landscapes of environmental photography, all the while distilling herself as the occasional poet.

Gavin Ivey

Born in Lismore New South Wales, Gavin (aka NAIAN) is a proud Bundjalung South Sea Islander man with an extensive background in community radio and arts, having been involved with the community radio sector for over 20 years. A graduate of NAISDA Dance College, Sydney; Moving Into Dance, Johannesburg; and The Australian Ballet School, Melbourne; Gavin has shared and danced extensively around Australia and internationally.

He has been a board member at the Community Media Training Organisation, First Nations Media Australia (FMNA), Positive Life New South Wales, and Gadigal Information Services Aboriginal Corporation, having also sat on the following panels — FNMA Content Sharing Advisory Committee, FNMA Indigitube Advisory Committee, 2020 FNMA First Sounds Music Compilation, 2019/2020 CBAA National Features and Documentary Series, and 2018 Spotify First Nations Sound Up Panel. Some appointments have included — Coordinator of 2015 First Nations Mardi Gras Parade entry, coordinator of 2017 Koori Radio Bluesfest/Boomerang Outside Broadcast, and Program Manager at Koori Radio, having hosted on air programs at Koori Radio and also did a stint at Bay FM in Byron Bay. Gavin also loves to DJ under the alias NAIAN, and plays regularly at various community and corporate events. Gavin also produces The Drift Zone, outLOUD and Seeds of Change Podcasts and has worked on numerous community audio projects.

Colin Kinchela

Colin is a Gomeroi Artist, Storyteller and Transformational Ethical Storytelling designer and facilitator, currently residing on the Lands of the Burramattagal.

Colin has over 20 years' experience working across the Arts sector as an Actor, Writer and Director with an avid interest in how stories are created and told. After working across TV, Film and Theatre, Colin now dedicates his time to educating others on the principles of Transformational Ethical Storytelling through Our Race. (www.ourrace.com.au)

As a strong advocate for First Nations' led storytelling, Colin has become a lead designer and facilitator of Transformational Ethical Storytelling.

In this role, Colin brings his wealth of experience working across the Arts sector to ensure all of Our Race's projects and partnerships have strong cultural safety protocols embedded from the beginning. He has played an integral role in the development of the Transformational Ethical Storytelling framework, which has included collaboration with Story Holders, advocacy groups and law firms Terri Janke and Company and Marque Lawyers.

Colin's passionate about changing how First Nations' stories are constructed and told and believes in the strength of genuine collaboration and creating safer spaces wherever stories are told.

Laniyuk

Laniyuk is a Larrakia, Kungarakan, Gurindji, and French writer and performer of poetry, memoir and fiction. She contributed to the book *Colouring the Rainbow: Blak, Queer and Trans Perspectives* (2015), has been published online, as well as in print poetry collections such as UQP's 2019 *Solid Air* and 2020 *Fire Front*. She has published speculative fiction through UQP's *This All Come Back Now* (2022) and Fremantle Arts Centre Press and Djed Press's *Unlimited Futures*. Her forthcoming poetry collection will be published by Magabala Books in 2023.

Tyberius Larking

Tyberius Larking is a Mirning and South Asian visual artist and poet living on Kaurna Country. As a man of trans experience, his work is heavily influenced by queer language and aesthetics and by the politics and history of Aboriginal queerness.

Gary Lee

Gary Lee (b. 1952) is a Larrakia artist from Darwin whose practice has involved photography, fashion design, curating, illustration/design and writing. He was the first Aboriginal student of visual arts at the Sydney College of the Arts in 1982 however he left after a year to pursue fashion design. He eventually returned to the Northern Territory to work in Aboriginal art which led him to a degree in anthropology. During his studies he honed his curating and writing skills through internships at the Australian Institute of Aboriginal Studies and the then Australian National Gallery.

Gary has written extensively on his photo-portrait practice, on the work of fellow artists, for curatorial projects, on Larrakia-related issues and Darwin history, and as part of his HIV-AIDS-related research for Darwin and national organisations. He wrote the play *Keep Him My Heart – A Larrakia-Filipino Love Story* (1993) to commemorate Darwin Aboriginal-Asian connections. He has conducted and participated in writing workshops in Australia and overseas. His inclusion in this anthology marks his debut as a published poet.

As a visual artist Gary has held numerous solo exhibitions in Australia and overseas and participated in significant national and international touring group exhibitions. His work is held in public collections including at the National Gallery of Australia, the National Gallery of Victoria and the Art Gallery of Western Australia. In 2022 he was awarded the Work on Paper Award at the Telstra National Aboriginal and Torres Strait Islander Awards, the Museum and Art Gallery Northern Territory, Darwin.

Neika Lehman

Neika Lehman (they/them) is a writer and member of this mob art collective. Neika grew up in nipaluna | Hobart and descends from the Trawlwoolway peoples of Tebrakunna Country. Their ancestors shape the loops in Neika's poetry, creative nonfiction and occasional art practice, exploring the tensions between memory, desire and time in settler colonies. Neika is grateful to the Kulin Nation on whose land they reside.

Lay Maloney

Lay Maloney is a queer, genderfluid storyteller of the Gumbaynggirr and Gunggandji First Nations and of South Sea Islander heritage.

They were born in Far North Queensland and grew up on the Mid North Coast before moving to Naarm to study in 2017.

Currently they work part-time as the Project Officer at the National Indigenous Youth Education Coalition, and for the rest of their week they write stories, read until the AM, avoid phone calls, and cry over fictional characters.

Lay won the State Library of Queensland's 2022 black&write! Fellowship for their LGBTQIA+ Young Adult novel *Weaving Us Together*.

Vika Mana

Meleika AKA Vika Mana, descends from the Zagareb and Dauareb tribes of Mer Island and the village of Fahefa in Tonga. Vika, like those before her, is a storyteller with a mouth full of venom and honey. They've been telling stories since they knew how to extend their jaw and let it collapse, to fit in myths and legends. They tell, sing, rap and draw stories. Sometimes she lets her body gracefully rise and fall to the rhythms of the ocean and the beating of the drums in dance.

Since 2018, they've emerged into the writing scene with spoken word and truth-telling, which has won them a place in The Next Chapter with the Wheeler Centre, Spotify Sound Up, Signal Boost, and the first nations program with Instagram and Screen Australia. They've been published in three anthologies, *Fire Front*, *Unlimited Futures* and *Poetry Unbound; 50 Poems to Open Your World*.

Elijah Manis

I am Elijah Manis, I am a First Nations Gay Torres Strait Islander man from Poruma and Masig Island. I am an artist of poetry and acting. I am the National NAIDOC Youth Award recipient for 2022 and was awarded for my history in activism, standing for LGBTQIA+ rights and for social justice. I attended the Murri school in Brisbane, graduating in 2021, and later completed a traineeship in Allied Health with IUIH (Institute for Urban Indigenous Health). I was raised by my single mother, by my grandmother, and my older sister. I have faced an upbringing with multiple forms of abuse, poverty, homelessness, depression and anxiety. My power and ability to express myself lies in poetry, revealing my love, translating my pain through a passion for words. My love for acting was influenced by Japanese professional wrestling (Puroresu) that has fascinated me my entire life. As a creative person I access the darkness of my experiences and create light and bring hope. My poetry connects with philosophy, spirituality, romance, culture and sexuality.

Ari Mills

I grew up on Larrakia Country under the stern warmth of the humid sun and garden sprinkler showers. There is where I situate my knowledge of love and community, there is where I learnt love can be soft and tough, altogether. My Mob are the Nangu and Kuku Yalanji Peoples. I admit that I still have much to learn and nurture with my Mob. This relationship, though, is a lifelong commitment. With any and all of my works contributing to a never-ending love letter to my People.

I have been studying a Bachelor of Arts in Criminology and International Politics down here in Naarm, on Boon Wurrung and Wurundjeri Country. This Country has cared for me in times when I wasn't able to do so myself – I'm forever grateful for the love I have gotten to harvest here.

My interests include the work in abolition, queerness and overall studies of love and connenction found within community. I dabble in many modes of artistic expression such as; drawing, writing, singing, makeup, drag and fashion etc. Many concepts I express in these mediums always come back to love, Black love, Queer Black love and familial Black love.

What's next?

After achieving the two goals I set this year (public speaking & publishing a piece of my work), I'd wish to perform some of my pieces for an audience, preferably for Mob. My next goal is to perform for an event with all Mob creatives to showcase our talents.

Jazz Money

Jazz Money is a poet and artist of Wiradjuri and Irish heritage producing works that encompass installation, digital, performance, film and print. Their writing has been widely published nationally and internationally and performed on stages around the world. Jazz's first poetry collection, the best-selling *how to make a basket* (UQP, 2021) was the 2020 winner of the David Unaipon Award. In 2022 Jazz was a recipient of the prestigious Dreaming Award from the Australia Council for the Arts for her work with poetry. As a cross-disciplinary artist their work has been presented at: HeK Basel, Switzerland; The Shed, New York; Pivô, São Paulo; Palais de Tokyo, Paris; Museum of Contemporary Art Australia; ACMI, Melbourne; Powerhouse MAAS, Sydney; Carriageworks, Sydney; the Fremantle Biennale; and the Hyphenated Biennale.

Alita Morgan

Alita Morgan is a Yorta Yorta, Wamba Wamba and Barapa Barapa transwoman. She is also descended from the Ngati Rangiwewehi iwi of the Te Arawa waka across the ditch in Aotearoa. She was born on Dharug country and has spent most of her life living on Kameygal, Gadigal or Dharug country.

Ellen van Neerven

Ellen van Neerven is a writer and editor. Their mother is Mununjali from the Yugambeh Nation and their father is Dutch from Mierlo, North Brabant. Ellen's books include *Heat and Light*, *Comfort Food* and *Throat*.

Ellen O'Brien

Ellen O'Brien is a Garigal/Walkeloa writer living on Gadigal land. Ellen is the 2022 Program Officer for The Writing Zone and a junior editor at the *Sydney Review of Books*. Her prose and poetry has been published in *Sydney Review of Books, Meanjin, Overland, Rabbit, Cordite* and *un Magazine*. She was previously a facilitator for the Feminist Killjoys Reading Group.

Steven Oliver

Steven Oliver is a descendant of the Kuku-Yalanji, Waanyi, Gangalidda, Woppaburra, Bundjalung and Biripi peoples. He became notorious with ABC's Black Comedy as a writer/actor/associate producer where his creations 'The Tiddas' helped gain him a FAVOURITE COMEDY PERFORMER OF THE DECADE finalist nomination at the 2020 AACTAs.

Other TV roles include Indigenous Arts Quiz Show Faboriginal for which he was creator/writer/presenter, writer/presenter on the documentary *Looky Looky Here Comes Cooky*. He has also featured in critically acclaimed documentaries *Occupation Native* and *History Bites Back*. His web series A Chance Affair was nominated for best web series at the 2018 LGBTQIA+ Australian Awards and Screen Producers Australia Awards.

His poetry is published in national and international poetry journals such as *Ora Nui, Australian Poetry Journal, Solid Air, Admissions, Firefront* and also the Institute For Modern Art's publication of *Making Art Work*. His plays *Proppa Solid* and *From Darkness* are published by Playlab.

His cabaret show premiering at the 2019 Adelaide Cabaret Festival, *Bigger & Blacker* has since played at La Boite Theatre Brisbane, Sydney Opera House, Malthouse Theatre Melbourne, Adelaide Fringe Festival, Perth International Cabaret Festival, Darwin Festival and Belco Arts Canberra. He co-hosted the 2022 Sydney Mardi Gras for the ABC, the 2022 National NAIDOC Awards and the National Indigenous Music Awards for NITV/SBS Viceland.

Sandy O'Sullivan

Sandy O'Sullivan is a transgender/non-binary Wiradjuri person and Professor of Indigenous Studies in the Centre for Global Indigenous Futures on the Wallumattagal campus of Macquarie University, where they are a 2020-2024 ARC Future Fellow with a project titled Saving Lives: Mapping the influence of Indigenous LGBTIQ+ creative artists. The project explores the unique contribution of queer artists to understand how modelling complex identities contributes to the wellbeing of all First Nations Peoples.

Since 1991 they have taught and researched across gender and sexuality, museums, the body, performance, creativities and First Nations' identity. In addition to their academic work, Sandy has been a musician, performer and soundtext artist since 1982, holding national and international arts residencies.

Luke Patterson

Luke Patterson is a Gamilaroi poet, folklorist and musician living on Gadigal lands. His poetry has appeared in *Cordite*, *Plumwood Mountain*, *Rabbit*, *Running Dog* and *The Suburban Review*. He has also featured in the anthologies *Active Aesthetics*, *Firefront: first nation's poetry and power today* and *Best of Australian Poems 2021*. His research and creative pursuits are grounded in extensive work with First Nations and other community-based organisations across Australia.

Keith Quayle

Keith Quayle is a Malyangapa and Barkindji gay man from the corner countries of western New South Wales, living on Dharug country. His lived experience of the carceral system informs the work he carries out on behalf of people in contact with the criminal justice system and advocates for transformative change that will bring justice to those affected.

Steven Lindsay Ross

Steven Lindsay Ross is Wamba Wamba with cultural and familial connections to the Wiradjuri, Mutthi Mutthi and Gundidjtmara peoples. Steven works doing engagement and strategy in local government and is also a published writer, curator and producer.

Latoya Aroha Rule

Latoya Aroha Rule (1992) (they/ them) is a Takatāpui (Queer) & non-binary person who descends from Wiradjuri & Te Ātiawa peoples. Latoya grew up on Kaurna Country and in 2021 they moved to Gadigal Land where they study and work at Jumbunna Institute, University of Technology Sydney (UTS).

Latoya has focused their life on advocating against state-sanctioned violence and deaths in custody, instead urging toward abolition and decolonisation. They arrive at specific themes in their work especially from the experience of losing their elder brother Wayne Fella Morrison in custody in South Australia after he was brutally restrained with a spit hood. In 2022 Latoya helped establish the national #BanSpithoods Coalition, following the success of 'Fella's Bill' — the South Australian ban on spit hoods a year prior which was led by Latoya and their family.

Latoya also appreciates creative outputs that provide them and others opportunity for truth-telling and healing. They have featured in *Time Magazine*, *The Washington Post*, *Rolling Stone* magazine, on CBS Network and Four Corners, and have contributed their work to spaces such as the Art Gallery of New South Wales, the Art Gallery of South Australia and ACE Gallery, and in exhibitions in New York, Berlin and the UK. They look forward to curating their next work in a standalone exhibition, and distributing their critical doctoral research creatively through podcasting as a platform.

Jacyn de Santis

Acclaimed playwright, director, actor and multidisciplinary creative practitioner and performer, Jacyn De Santis has over twenty years of arts industry experience both on stage and behind the scenes. With connections from the desert to the sea, Jacyn belongs to Tiwi, Jawoyn, Katyeyte and Warlpiri Country. They are fluent in the Tiwi language and English, with strong conversational knowledge of Creole and Kunwinngu.

Their vast skill-set arises from national experience across remote and urban settings in festival and theatre production, writing, performing arts, puppetry, television, film, First Nations community service delivery and more. Jacyn has been widely recognised for being 'a real talent' (*The Australian*) and their nationally acclaimed theatre production, *Wulamanayuwi and the Seven Pamanui*, is the first ever piece of Tiwi contemporary theatre to be written and produced and was shortlisted for two Helpmann Awards in 2014. Jacyn currently lives in Mparntwe Alice Springs, Northern Territory.

Kirli Saunders

Kirli Saunders (OAM) is a proud Gunai Woman and award-winning multidisciplinary artist and consultant. Kirli was the New South Wales Aboriginal Woman of the Year (2020). In 2022, she was awarded an Order of Australia Medal for her contribution to the arts, particularly literature.

Her celebrated books include *The Incredible Freedom Machines* (Scholastic, 2018), *Kindred* (Magabala, 2019), *Bindi* (Magabala, 2020), *Our Dreaming* (Scholastic, 2022) and *Returning* (forthcoming Magabala Books, 2023). Among other awards, her books have been widely recognised in the Prime Minister's and Premier's Literary Awards in New South Wales, Queensland, Victoria and Western Australia. She has seven forthcoming titles.

Kirli's writing features in magazines and journals including *Vogue*, *Overland*, *Kill Your Darlings* and as public art with Red Room Poetry, AESOP and The Royal Botanic Gardens, Victoria. Her debut play, directed by Shari Sebbens, *Going Home* was supported by Playwriting Australia (2022) and following a second development will take the stage in 2023.

Her art has been commissioned by Google, Fender X Children's Ground, local and state government and regional galleries in New South Wales, and Western

Australia. Kirli's Solo Exhibition, RETURNING was supported by AUSCO (2022). As an artist, she collaborated with Kamsani Bin Salleh for VIVID, with TRACES thanks to Google and Magabala Books at Sydney Opera House.

Alison Whittaker

Alison Whittaker is a Gomeroi poet and academic.

Special thanks

Arlie Alizzi

The author of this collection's Foreword, is a Yugambeh (Kombumerri) trans man who lives on Yawuru Country in Broome. He is a writer, researcher and editor.

With thanks

We would like to thank all the Poets for their passion, work and contribution.

We would like to thank the many people and organisations that have supported and contributed to the development of this publication and the outLOUD First Nations LGBTQIA+ SB Story and Writing project, including:

- BlaQ Aboriginal Corporation
- First Nations Australia Media Association
- Sydney WorldPride
- Dr Elizabeth Harris AM and Prof. Mark Harris AO
- Pride Foundation Australia
- Lesbians Incorporated
- City of Sydney (cultural grants program)
- Copyright Agency Cultural Fund
- Special Counsel Ian McDonald and the staff at SIMPSONS
- Damien Webb and the Indigenous Engagement Team at the State Library of NSW
- Australian Society of Authors and Authors Legal
- Tranby Staff and Volunteers

THANKS

Notes on Sources

Carp • Alison Whittaker
First published in *Cordite Poetry Review*, issue 88, *TRANSQUEER*, November 2018

Colonial fetish – Part 1. • by Latoya Aroha Rule
First exhibited during 2021 for TRANS* FUTURES ARCHIVE at ISCP
(International Studio & Curatorial Program) in Brooklyn, New York

Fam is Blak • Latoya Aroha Rule
First published by Art Gallery of New South Wales in response to the exhibition
'Family: Visions of a Shared Humanity' (2021-22) Guest curated by Franklin Sirmans,
the director of the Pérez Art Museum Miami (PAMM)

#mardigrasrainbowdreaming • Jazz Money
First published in *unMagazine*, issue 15.1, *Surplus*, ed. Snack Syndicate, 2021;
also in *Best of Australian Poems 2021*, ed. Ellen van Neerven & Toby Fitch,
Australian Poetry, 2022

Pieman Heads • Neika Lehman
First published in *Cordite Poetry Review*, issue 103, *AMBLE*, October 2021

redbellyblacksnake • Jazz Money
First published in *Australian Poetry Journal*, issue 9.1, *Resist*, ed. John Kinsella, 2019
and subsequently in *how to make a basket*, UQP, 2021

un_domesticated • Yvette Henry Holt
First published in *Cordite Poetry Review*, issue 89, *DOMESTIC*, February 2019

You can't pray the Gay out of me • Kirli Saunders
From the forthcoming *Returning*, Kirli Saunders, Magabala Books, 2023